ANIMAL OPPOSITES

Mark Carwardine

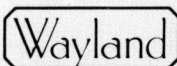

Titles in this series
Noisy and Quiet Animals
Daytime and Night-time Animals
Quick and Slow Animals

First published in 1988 by

Wayland (Publishers) Ltd.
61 Western Road, Hove
East Sussex BN3 1JD
England

© Copyright 1988 Ilex Publishers Limited

British Library Cataloguing in Publication Data

Carwardine, Mark
　Big and small animals.—
　(Animal opposites).
　1. Animals—Juvenile literature
　I. Title　II. Series
　591　　QL49

ISBN 1-85210-296-9

Created and produced by
Ilex Publishers Ltd
29–31 George Street
Oxford OX1 2AJ

Designed by Paul Richards, Designers and Partners, Oxford

Illustrations by Martin Camm, Jim Channell
and John Francis
Bernard Thornton Artists

Printed in Spain by Gráficas Estella, S. A.

Cover illustration by Jim Channell
a giraffe and a harvest mouse

Contents

Hippopotamus	4
Hummingbird	6
Blue whale	8
Bat-eared fox	10
Giraffe	12
Elephant shrew	14
Ostrich	16
Harvest mouse	18
Elephant	20
Dik-dik	22
Further information	24

The hippo is a big animal.

It is one of the biggest and noisiest animals in Africa. This hippo is holding its breath while it runs along the bottom of a river.

The hummingbird is a small animal.

It is so small that it can poke its head inside flowers to drink the nectar.
This hummingbird is hovering in front of a flower.

The blue whale is a big animal.

It is bigger than any other animal that has ever lived on earth.
This blue whale has a giant-sized baby.

The bat-eared fox is a small animal.

It is one of the smallest foxes in the world. This bat-eared fox has caught a locust for its breakfast.

The giraffe is a big animal.

It is taller than any other animal in the world.
This giraffe is stretching its long neck to eat the leaves in a tree.

The elephant shrew is a small animal.

It eats beetles, spiders, millipedes and other creepy crawlies.
This elephant shrew has a very long nose.

The ostrich is a big animal.

It is so big and heavy that it cannot fly.
This ostrich has swallowed a huge bundle of leaves.

The harvest mouse is a small animal.

It is so small and light that it can climb to the top of a grass stem.
This harvest mouse is scrambling around in the grass like a little monkey.

The elephant is a big animal.

It has enormous ears, big teeth and a very long, bendy nose.
This elephant lives in India.

The dik-dik is a small animal.

It likes to eat leaves and grass.
This dik-dik is hiding under a bush where it cannot be seen.